WE LOV GLASSES

This book uses OpenDyslexic font.

Written by Stephanie Lipsey-Liu

Illustrated by Viktoria Soltis-Doan

MW01136547

For my daughter, Isabella

First printed 2022

ISBN 978-1-7399336-9-2
Little Lion Publishing UK
Nottingham, England
www.facebook.com/littlelionpublishing

Little Lion Publishing UK

Contents

Short-sighted....................page 2

Long-sighted....................page 4

Astigmatism....................page 6

Anisometropia....................page 8

Squint....................page 10

Bifocals for children.........page 12

Myopia management........page 14

UV protection....................page 16

Coloured lenses..................page 18

Low vision aids..................page 20

FAQs....................page 24

Glossary....................page 27

Optical illusions..................page 28

I love MY glasses because they help
me to see the board at school clearly.

Lou

Lou can see close things (like this apple) very well, but things that are far away look blurry without glasses (like the tree).

Lou is "myopic", otherwise known as short-sighted.

If you are short-sighted, it is a good idea to wear your glasses all the time and spend lots of time outdoors.

Not wearing your glasses or under-correcting a short-sighted prescription can make you more short-sighted even faster! So this is not a good idea.

A short-sighted glasses prescription will start with a minus sign. For example:

High amounts of short-sightedness also increases the risk of some serious eye conditions. Luckily there are now glasses to help slow down how quickly short-sight progresses!

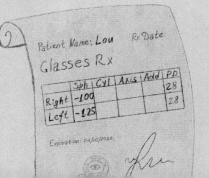

Patient Name: Lou   Rx Date:

Glasses Rx

	Sph	Cyl	Axis	Add	PD
Right	-1.00				28
Left	-1.25				28

Expiration: 04/20/2022

I love MY glasses because they stop my head from hurting.

4

Bobbi is "hypermetropic", otherwise known as long-sighted. Small amounts of long-sight are normal in children and do not usually need correcting.

Bobbi's glasses can help with headaches caused from having moderate to high amounts of long-sight.

All children use muscles in their eyes to change the focus of the natural lens inside their eyes to be able to see close up. This is called accommodation. Long-sighted children have to accommodate to see far away as well as close up. If there is a lot of long-sight then this can be corrected so there is less strain on the eye muscles.

A long-sighted glasses prescription will start with a plus. For example:

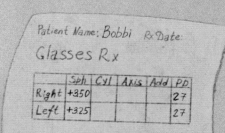

Patient Name: Bobbi   Rx Date:

Glasses Rx

	Sph	Cyl	Axis	Add	PD
Right	+350				27
Left	+325				27

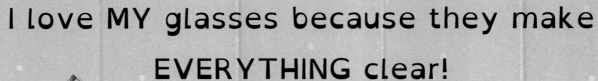

I love MY glasses because they make EVERYTHING clear!

Sam has "astigmatism", which means his vision is always a bit blurry without his glasses.

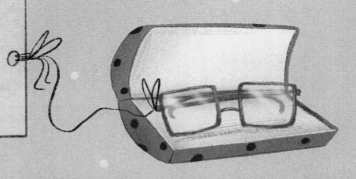

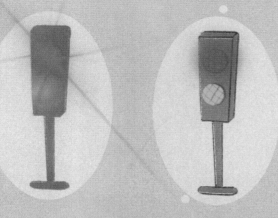

Astigmatism is sometimes explained as having "rugby ball-shaped eyes". This is not entirely accurate as it is only the cornea and/or the lens that are slightly more curved in one direction than the other, a bit like a rugby ball.

Astigmatism is where each eye has two separate focal points. This means nothing is completely in focus without glasses. It can also cause eye strain and sometimes double vision if it is not corrected.

Small amounts of astigmatism are common. Astigmatism can occur alongside short-sight or long-sight.

An example of an astigmatic prescription:

Patient Name: Sam   Rx Date:

Glasses Rx

	Sph	Cyl	Axis	Add	PD
Right	+0.50	-1.25	180		26
Left	+1.00	-2.00	170		26

7

I love MY glasses because they help my left eye see as well as my right eye.

Theo has "anisometropia". One of his eyes is more long-sighted than the other by more than +1.00.

Some children may need a patch on their good eye for a limited time a day if the bad eye doesn't improve with glasses alone.

My Reward Chart
My name is _Theo_

Sunday	⭐
Monday	🙂
Tuesday	🙂
Wednesday	😊
Thursday	🙂
Friday	🙂
Saturday	🙂

Sometimes children who have a big difference in each eye, won't notice much difference, even with their glasses on. This is because they can often see very well with their good eye.

If a child is long-sighted and has one eye stronger than the other, this must be corrected before 8 years old, otherwise the bad eye will never see properly.

An example of a prescription with anisometropia:

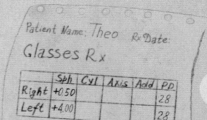

Patient Name: Theo   Rx Date:
Glasses Rx

	Sph	Cyl	Axis	Add	PD
Right	+0.50				28
Left	+4.00				28

9

I love MY glasses because they
help me to see in 3D!

Ruby

Ruby has a type of "squint" or turn which means one eye turns in towards her nose when she isn't using her glasses. This is an "esotropia".

Without her glasses, Ruby only uses the eye facing forwards properly. Glasses help to make both eyes look forwards so she can see things in 3D.

Some children with squints may never see in 3D, even when both eyes look forwards. Children who don't have good 3D vision will not be able to watch 3D films, they will just see two blurry images.

Some squints can't be fully corrected with glasses and may need an operation.

Some children may have a squint where their eye turns outwards instead of inwards. This is called an "exotropia".

I love MY glasses because I can see
my writing better.

Louis has bifocals which help him see things up close.

Accommodation problems are common in children with Down syndrome and other learning disabilities. It's important to wear glasses for this problem to see food, toys and writing properly.

Children who have had cataracts removed will also need bifocal or varifocal glasses.
On a glasses prescription, the "add" is how much extra is added for seeing close up.

An example of a prescription that might need bifocals:

Patient Name: Louis   Rx Date:

Glasses Rx

	Sph	Cyl	Axis	Add	PD
Right	+2.00			+3.00	
Left	+3.00			+3.00	

We love OUR glasses because they are the latest technology in glasses lenses!

Niamh and Anna

14

Short-sighted eyeballs are often longer than normal which can increase the risk of some eye problems.

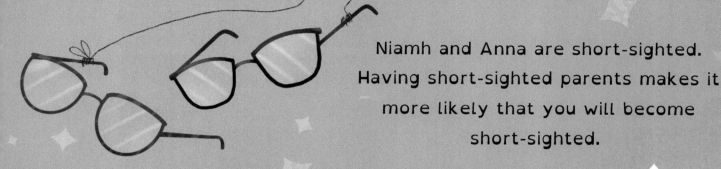

MiYOSMART glasses help slow down how fast short-sight progresses and try and stop the eye growing as long as it might have without MiYOSMART.

Niamh and Anna are short-sighted. Having short-sighted parents makes it more likely that you will become short-sighted.

MiYOSMART lenses can be worn by any child with a short-sighted prescription up to -10.00. The lenses are toughened, have an anti-glare coating and UV blocker. The aim is to slow down or stop the progression of short-sight. Ask your optician about MiYOSMART.

It is estimated that half of the population will be short-sighted by the year 2050!

Example of a prescription with a high amount of short-sight:

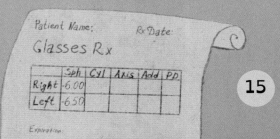

Patient Name: Rx Date:

Glasses Rx

	Sph	Cyl	Axis	Add	PD
Right	-6.00				
Left	-6.50				

Expiration:

I love MY glasses because they protect
my eyes from ultraviolet light.

Isabella

Isabella's glasses block out the ultraviolet rays from the sun and protect her eyes and the thin eyelid skin. Like how sun cream protects your skin on the rest of your body.

You can get clear or tinted lenses to help block out the sun's ultraviolet (UV) rays. You can even get lenses that change from clear to tinted in the sun. These will filter out the UV even when they are clear. If your glasses have lenses that have been made thinner, this will automatically block out UV too.

Filtering out UV light is important because conditions such as cataracts and macula degeneration can be made worse by UV light. There are even some growths that can occur on the eyes and eyelids because of UV light!

I love MY glasses because they stop words from jumping around the page.

Josie

Josie's glasses have a special tint just for her to help her read more easily.

I Love My Glasses

I Love My Glasses

Without the coloured tint, to Josie it looks like words move around the page. The colour helps the words stay still for Josie and stop her eyes from straining.

Problems with words moving, looking wobbly or flickering can be associated with conditions like ADD/ADHD, dyslexia, Meares-Irlen syndrome, autism and dyspraxia.

Children who use these glasses have often used a coloured overlay first. A colourimetry assessment will find the exact colour for your glasses and can be a different colour to the overlay.

I love MY glasses because they read for me!

George has an eye condition called nystagmus which means his eyes move side to side very quickly and he can't see well enough to read. There are many other eye conditions that can mean someone is unable to read without extra help. Sometimes magnifying glasses help enough to read but aren't always practical.

George's glasses have a special camera on the side. It can scan writing in front of him and read it out loud!

These glasses can be used for anyone who can't see well enough to read. Examples of the camera include OrCam and Envision.

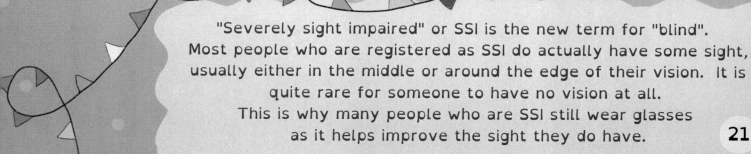

"Severely sight impaired" or SSI is the new term for "blind". Most people who are registered as SSI do actually have some sight, usually either in the middle or around the edge of their vision. It is quite rare for someone to have no vision at all. This is why many people who are SSI still wear glasses as it helps improve the sight they do have.

We ALL love

our glasses!

23

FAQs

What age should I take my child for an eye test?

Usually, age 4-5 is a good age for an eye test as children this age can usually cooperate well and start to read letters or numbers. However, children do not need to be able to read letters or numbers before having an eye test. Opticians have equipment that can be used to take vital measurements, even if the child can't read.

Reasons to go for an eye test under 4 years old.

Any signs of an eye turning in or out, a child whose eyes are constantly searching around or eyes that wobble very fast. Another reason would be any signs of a white reflection in the pupil which can be very serious. Also any child whose immediate family have eye problems including a squint or turn or high amounts of long or short-sight or other hereditary eye problems.

How often will my child need their eyes testing?

This will usually be 6 or 12 monthly. Sometimes for young children it can be 3 monthly or less if they are being monitored or treated for something.

How much is an eye test for a child?

If you live in the UK, then eye tests and basic glasses for under 16s are "free" - funded by the NHS. They remain free until age 18 if the young person is in full time education.

Will my child need glasses forever?

If they are short-sighted, then they will likely always need glasses to see far away. If they are long-sighted then they may only need glasses for close work or may need them full time as they get older. If they are wearing glasses to correct a lazy eye, once they get past 8 years old, they may not need them anymore. This would be something your optician will discuss with you.

How can you test a child with autism?

There are a few options for children with additional needs. One is to find an optician that is quieter and will allow either a longer appointment or a few separate shorter appointments. If there are obstacles like too much light or noise, then discuss this before the appointment. If going to an optician is too overwhelming then they may be able to have their eye test done at home. Look for an optician that offers home visits or can recommend someone who does. This will still be covered on the NHS (in the UK).

What is a lazy eye?

A lazy eye is an eye that, even with glasses on, cannot see as well as the other eye. This is often correctable up to age 8 by using glasses and/or a patch and in some cases an operation if there is an operable squint/turn as well as the lazy eye. Once this eye has improved and the child is older than 8, there is no risk of it becoming lazy again. However, if a lazy eye is treated and then treatment stops before aged 8, it can become lazy again very quickly. The same goes for patching the good eye. Too much patching and the good eye will become lazy. This is why children with a lazy eye are very closely monitored.

Will wearing glasses make my child's eyes worse or reliant on glasses?

The short answer is no. Glasses generally just correct your vision back to normal, as if there was no prescription. So wearing glasses too much isn't possible. The opposite can be true though, especially in children with a lazy eye or short-sight. Not wearing glasses can stop a lazy eye from improving and can make short-sight progress faster. If a child wants to wear glasses all the time but doesn't really need to, there is no harm in it as long as they are the correct prescription for them (not someone else's glasses).

What is myopia management?

Myopia management involves using glasses, contact lenses or eye drops to try to slow down how much a short-sighted eye is growing and reduce how short-sighted that child would end up. Myopia management glasses lenses include MiYOSMART from Hoya and Stellest™ from Essilor®. Contact lens options include MiSight® and NaturalVue®. Other options include orthokeratology and atropine treatment.

What can we do to help our short-sighted child?

Apart from using myopia control glasses or contact lenses, research has shown that more time outdoors and very good light indoors can slow down the progression of short-sight. Also limiting unnecessary close work and keeping close work at 30 cm or more if possible can help. Trying to take a break by looking into the distance every half an hour of close work can also help.

Glossary

Amblyopia: An eye that doesn't see properly even with full glasses correction. Also known as a lazy eye.

Anisometropia: A difference of more than 1.00 dioptres between the two eyes.

Astigmatism: When the lens or cornea or both are curved slightly more in one direction than the other, leading to one eye having two focal points. Usually correctable with glasses.

Esotropia: One eye turns inwards.

Exotropia: One eye turns outwards.

Hyperopic: Long-sighted. Children are usually hyperopic but moderate-to-high amounts will need correcting to reduce eye strain and improve vision, especially to help see things close up.

Myopic: Short-sighted. Without glasses, things that are far away appear blurry.

Severely sight impaired: Used to be known as blind. These people will have significantly reduced central or peripheral vision or both.

Sight impaired: Used to be known as partially sighted. These people will have reduced central or peripheral vision or both.

Optical illusions

How many black dots can you see?

How many black dots are really there?

You might be surprised to know, the answer is actually none!

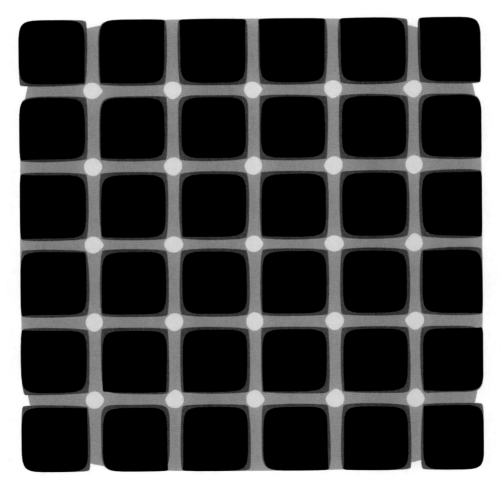

The scintillating grid

Which line is longer?

Why don't you measure them and find out?

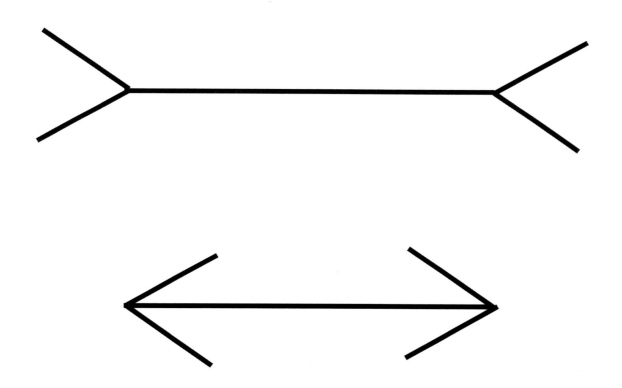

The answer is, they are actually both
the same length!

Design your own glasses

About the Author

Stephanie is an ophthalmic optician. She graduated from Cardiff University with a degree in Optometry in 2009. She completed her last year of training in Ipswich Hospital and has a special interest in myopia management. She co-owns a home visiting opticians and an independent practice in Nottingham.

About the Illustrator

Viktoria lives in Berlin. She is an international illustrator and writer of children's books. In her spare time she likes to do yoga, spend time with her husband and son, pick flowers and drink coffee.

Other books by Stephanie:

"A Fluffle of Bunnies and other fun collective nouns"

"A Waddle of Penguins and other fun collective nouns"

"Disaster at the Moordale Monster Parade"

"seffy the Dragon, Learns to Tell the Time"

Please leave us a review on Amazon.

Made in the USA
Las Vegas, NV
16 December 2023

82965869R00021